Future-Proofing Your Career

A roadmap for embracing change and adaptation

Roy S. Ferranti

Nathaniel Klein

Future-Proofing
Your
Career!

A roadmap for embracing change and
adaptation

By

Roy S. Ferranti
&
Nathaniel Klein

Table of Contents

Introduction

In an era defined by relentless change, our careers stand as both the compass and the canvas of our lives. The world of work is evolving at a breathtaking pace, driven by technological advances, shifting demographics, and global dynamics. To thrive in this ever-changing landscape, we must equip ourselves with the tools and mindset to not just weather change, but to embrace it, adapt to it, and emerge stronger than before.

"Future-Proofing Your Career: A Roadmap for Embracing Change and Adaptation" is a guide born from the necessity of our times. It's a call to action for anyone who understands that complacency is no longer an option. Whether you're a recent graduate embarking on your professional journey or a seasoned veteran looking to remain relevant, this book is your companion on the path to career resilience.

In this book, we'll embark on a transformative journey. We'll begin by dissecting the rapidly evolving work landscape, exploring the very forces reshaping industries and professions. From the rise of automation to the emergence of a gig economy, we'll decode the trends that demand our attention.

However, the heart of this roadmap lies in the development of a change-ready mindset. We'll delve into the psychology of adaptation, unraveling the power of a growth mindset and ways to conquer the fear of change.

Next, we'll embark on a journey of self-discovery, assessing our skills and strengths to build a personalized adaptation toolkit. Lifelong learning, networking, and skill development will be your allies in this endeavor.

With a strong foundation in place, we'll craft a resilience plan tailored to your aspirations, setting clear goals and plotting a flexible career path. You'll also learn how to thrive within your current workplace, fostering agility, innovation, and strong relationships.

As we explore the entrepreneurial mindset, you'll discover how to seize opportunities, innovate within your role, or even venture into the world of entrepreneurship.

In an increasingly digital world, we'll also explore the strategic use of technology for career advancement and how to overcome common career obstacles, from setbacks to workplace stress.

Throughout the book, you'll encounter real-life case studies, drawing inspiration and wisdom from individuals who have successfully navigated the challenges of change.

In the end, this book is not merely a read; it's a roadmap for action. It will equip you with the knowledge, tools, and inspiration to forge a career that's not just resilient but flourishing in the face of change. Your journey towards future-proofing your career starts here.

The Need for Career Resilience

In today's rapidly evolving world, the concept of a linear and predictable career path has become a relic of the past. The career landscape is no longer a stable, well-defined terrain; instead, it resembles a constantly shifting mosaic of opportunities and challenges. This transformation has given rise to an urgent need for career resilience.

Career resilience is the capacity to not only withstand the winds of change but also to harness them for personal and professional growth. It is the ability to adapt, learn, and thrive amidst uncertainty and disruption. Why is career resilience so crucial in the 21st century?

1. *The Pace of Change:* The pace of change in technology, industries, and job roles is unprecedented. What's considered cutting-edge today may be outdated in a matter of years or even months. Those who can't adapt risk being left behind.

2. *Economic Uncertainty:* Global economic shifts, recessions, and pandemics have demonstrated how fragile job security can be. Career resilience provides a safety net when unexpected disruptions occur.

3. *Lifelong Learning:* Continuous learning is no longer an option; it's a necessity. A resilient career requires a commitment to ongoing skill development and staying updated with industry trends.

4. *Diverse Career Paths:* Traditional career paths are giving way to more diverse and non-linear trajectories. Resilience allows individuals to pivot and explore new opportunities as they arise.

5. *Entrepreneurial Mindset:* An entrepreneurial mindset is increasingly valuable, whether you're running your own business or navigating within a larger organization. Career resilience encourages innovation and adaptability.

6. *Personal Fulfillment*: A resilient career isn't just about survival; it's about finding fulfillment and purpose in your work. Resilience enables you to align your career with your values and passions.

7. *Psychological Well-being*: The ability to adapt and bounce back from setbacks is closely tied to mental health. Career resilience fosters emotional well-being, reducing the stress of constant change.

8. Future-Proofing: In a world where jobs are automated and industries evolve rapidly, career resilience is the key to future-proofing your livelihood.

In essence, career resilience is not a luxury but a fundamental skill for thriving in the modern workplace. It empowers individuals to take control of their careers, navigate uncertainty with confidence, and seize opportunities that arise in an ever-changing world. This book, "Future-Proofing Your Career," is your guide to developing and harnessing the power of career resilience, equipping you to not only survive but flourish in the dynamic and unpredictable journey of your professional life.

Chapter 1

The Changing Work Landscape

The work landscape of the 21st century is undergoing a profound transformation, reshaping the way we think about careers and employment. Several powerful forces are converging to redefine traditional notions of work, creating both challenges and opportunities for individuals and organizations alike. To navigate this shifting terrain effectively, it's crucial to understand the key dynamics shaping the changing work landscape.

1. Technological Advancements: Perhaps the most conspicuous driver of change in the work landscape is technology. Automation, artificial intelligence (AI), machine learning, and robotics are rapidly altering how tasks are performed across industries. While this automation presents efficiencies and productivity gains, it also raises concerns about job displacement and the need for new skill sets.

2. Gig Economy and Freelancing: The rise of the gig economy has given birth to a workforce characterised by freelancers, independent contractors, and on-demand workers. Platforms like Uber, Airbnb, and Upwork have made it easier for individuals to monetize their skills and assets, offering flexibility but often lacking traditional employment benefits.

3. *Remote and Flexible Work:* Advancements in communication technology have made remote work more feasible and attractive. The COVID-19 pandemic accelerated this shift, prompting many companies to adopt remote work arrangements. Hybrid work models are becoming more prevalent, allowing employees to balance work with personal life.

4. *Globalisation*: Globalisation continues to connect economies and businesses worldwide. This interconnectedness has expanded opportunities for international collaboration but also intensified competition and the need for cross-cultural skills.

5. *Lifelong Learning:* The pace of change in the job market necessitates a commitment to lifelong learning. Professionals must continually acquire new skills and update existing ones to remain relevant. Education and training are no longer confined to the early stages of one's career; they are ongoing endeavors.

6. *Environmental and Social Concerns:* Environmental sustainability and social responsibility are increasingly influential in shaping corporate values and strategies. Companies are being held accountable for their impact on the planet and society, which is leading to changes in corporate culture and practices.

7. *Career Non-Linearity:* Traditional linear career paths are giving way to non-linear trajectories. Individuals are more likely to change careers multiple times in their lives, necessitating adaptability and a willingness to pivot.

8. *Hybrid Skills:* As technology continues to integrate with various industries, there is a growing demand for hybrid skills—combinations of technical and soft skills. These skills bridge the gap between human abilities and automation.

9. *Ageing Workforce:* In many developed countries, the workforce is ageing, which presents challenges related to retirement, succession planning, and age diversity in the workplace.

10. *Mental Health and Well-being:* The changing work landscape has implications for mental health. The blurring of boundaries between work and personal life in a digital world can lead to burnout and stress, prompting a greater focus on well-being initiatives.

11. *Inclusivity and Diversity:* There is a growing recognition of the importance of diversity and inclusion in the workplace. Companies are increasingly valuing diverse perspectives, backgrounds, and experiences as they understand the benefits they bring, including improved innovation and decision-making.

12. *E-commerce and the Digital Marketplace:* The rise of e-commerce and the digital marketplace has revolutionized retail and created new opportunities for entrepreneurs and small businesses. Online platforms have made it easier than ever to start and run a business, reaching global markets.

13. *Health and Well-being Focus:* The COVID-19 pandemic underscored the significance of health and well-being in the work landscape. Companies are investing in employee wellness programs, flexible work arrangements, and mental health support to foster a healthier, more resilient workforce.

14. *Ethical and Sustainable Business Practices:* Consumers are increasingly concerned about the ethical and sustainable practices of the companies they engage with. This has prompted a shift in corporate responsibility toward more sustainable and ethical business models.

15. Data-Driven Decision-Making: Data analytics and artificial intelligence have enabled organisations to make more informed decisions. Professionals who can analyze and interpret data are in high demand across various industries.

16. Urbanization and Remote Work: The changing work landscape has implications for urbanization. As remote work becomes more common, people have greater flexibility in choosing where to live, potentially reshaping urban and rural demographics.

17. Entrepreneurship and Innovation:

Entrepreneurship is no longer confined to startups. Many established organizations are fostering cultures of innovation, encouraging employees to explore new ideas and initiatives.

18. Government Policies and Regulations:

Government policies and regulations play a significant role in shaping the work landscape. Changes in labor laws, taxation, immigration policies, and trade agreements can have profound effects on industries and employment.

19. Cybersecurity and Privacy: With the increasing digitization of business operations, cybersecurity and data privacy have become critical concerns. Professionals with expertise in these

areas are in high demand to protect sensitive information.

20. *Aging Population and Retirement Trends:* The aging population in many countries is impacting retirement trends and workforce dynamics. Companies are exploring strategies to retain and utilize the knowledge and experience of older workers.

Navigating the changing work landscape requires adaptability, resilience, and a willingness to embrace new opportunities and challenges. It also demands a commitment to staying informed about emerging trends and technologies. Those who can harness the transformative forces at play and position themselves effectively will be better equipped to thrive in this dynamic and evolving professional world.

Understanding Future Trends

In a world where change is the only constant, understanding and anticipating future trends is a vital skill for individuals and organizations alike. The ability to recognize emerging developments, whether they pertain to technology, industries, or society, can provide a competitive advantage and help individuals make informed decisions about their careers. Here's a closer look at the importance of understanding future trends and some strategies for doing so:

1. Staying Relevant: One of the primary reasons to understand future trends is to stay relevant in your chosen field. As technology advances and industries evolve, certain skills and knowledge become obsolete while others gain prominence. By anticipating these shifts, you can proactively acquire the skills and expertise needed to remain competitive in the job market.

2. *Seizing Opportunities:* Future trends often create new opportunities. For example, emerging technologies can lead to the creation of entirely new industries and job roles. Those who can identify these opportunities early can position themselves to take advantage of them, whether it's starting a new venture or transitioning to a high-demand career path.

3. *Mitigating Risks:* Conversely, understanding future trends can also help individuals and organizations mitigate risks. Anticipating potential challenges, such as industry disruptions or economic downturns, allows for proactive planning and risk management strategies.

4. *Innovation and Problem-Solving*: Being aware of future trends fosters a mindset of innovation and problem-solving. When you can foresee upcoming challenges or customer needs, you're better equipped to develop innovative solutions and products that address those needs.

5. Career Resilience: Understanding future trends is a key component of career resilience. It enables you to adapt to changing circumstances, pivot when necessary, and make informed decisions about your career path.

Strategies for Understanding Future Trends:

1. **Continuous Learning**: Make learning a lifelong habit. Stay curious and seek out information about emerging technologies, industry trends, and societal changes. Attend workshops, take online courses, and read relevant books and articles.
2. **Networking**: Connect with professionals in your field and related industries. Engaging in meaningful conversations with a diverse group of people can provide valuable insights into trends and opportunities.
3. **Industry Research**: Regularly research your industry or area of interest. Follow industry publications, reports, and thought leaders.

Join industry-specific forums or groups to stay informed.

4. *Scenario Planning:* Consider various scenarios for the future, both positive and negative. This exercise can help you prepare for different outcomes and make contingency plans.

5. *Mentorship*: Seek out mentors or advisors who have a deep understanding of your field. They can offer guidance and share their insights into future trends.

6. *Data Analysis*: Leverage data and analytics to identify emerging trends. Data-driven decision-making is becoming increasingly essential in various industries.

7. *Cross-Disciplinary Learning:* Explore topics beyond your immediate field of expertise. Sometimes, insights and innovations emerge at the intersection of different disciplines.

Understanding future trends is a dynamic and ongoing process. It requires a proactive and curious mindset, a commitment to learning, and the flexibility to adapt to changing circumstances. By honing this skill, you can position yourself for success in an ever-evolving world.

Chapter 2

Embracing Change

Change is a force of nature in our modern world, and nowhere is it more evident than in the realm of work and careers. Embracing change is not merely a choice; it's an imperative for those who seek to thrive in this dynamic landscape. In the context of the book "Future-Proofing Your Career," understanding how to embrace change is the cornerstone of building career resilience. Here's why:

1. Change as a Constant: Change is not an occasional disruption; it's the new normal. Rapid advancements in technology, economic shifts, and global events have accelerated the pace of change. Those who resist change risk becoming obsolete.

2. Adaptability and Agility: Embracing change fosters adaptability and agility, two critical traits for career resilience. When you're open to change, you can pivot quickly, acquire new skills, and adjust to new circumstances, giving you a competitive edge.

3. Innovation and Creativity: Change often brings opportunities for innovation and creativity. Embracing change encourages you to think outside the box, explore new ideas, and seek novel solutions to emerging challenges.

4. Overcoming Fear: The fear of change is a common human emotion. However, by understanding change and its potential benefits, you can overcome this fear and approach new situations with confidence.

5. Learning and Growth: Change provides fertile ground for learning and personal growth. Each new experience and challenge is an opportunity to acquire new knowledge, develop skills, and broaden your horizons.

6. Resilience in Uncertainty: In uncertain times, those who embrace change are more resilient.

They can navigate ambiguity with greater ease, make informed decisions in complex situations, and bounce back from setbacks.

7. Seizing Opportunities: Change often brings unexpected opportunities. Whether it's a new job opening, a chance to pivot your career, or a groundbreaking innovation, those who embrace change are more likely to seize these opportunities when they arise.

Strategies for Embracing Change:

1. *Cultivate a Growth Mindset:* Adopt a mindset that sees challenges as opportunities for growth. Believe in your ability to learn and adapt to new circumstances.
2. *Stay Informed:* Keep up with industry trends, technological advancements, and global events that could impact your career. Knowledge is a powerful tool for navigating change.

3. **Set Clear Goals**: Define your career goals and aspirations, but remain flexible in how you achieve them. Having a sense of direction can help you make purposeful changes.
4. ***Network and Collaborate:*** Build a strong professional network. Collaborate with others who can offer diverse perspectives and support during times of change.
5. ***Continuous Learning:*** Commit to lifelong learning. Take courses, attend workshops, and seek opportunities to acquire new skills and knowledge.
6. ***Mindfulness and Resilience Training:*** Practices like mindfulness and resilience training can help you manage stress and stay grounded during times of change.

Cultivating a Growth Mindset

In the journey of future-proofing your career, cultivating a growth mindset is like nurturing the fertile soil from which all your professional growth will spring. Coined by psychologist Carol Dweck, a growth mindset is the belief that abilities and intelligence can be developed through dedication, learning, and hard work. In contrast, a fixed mindset assumes that abilities are innate and unchangeable.

Here's why cultivating a growth mindset is pivotal for your career resilience and success:

1. *Embracing Challenges:* Individuals with a growth mindset view challenges as opportunities to learn and grow. They don't shy away from difficulties; instead, they embrace them as stepping stones to improvement. In your career, this means you'll tackle complex projects with enthusiasm, seeing them as chances to enhance your skills.

2. *Overcoming Setbacks:* A growth mindset enables you to bounce back from setbacks. Instead of seeing failure as a dead end, you perceive it as a detour on the road to success. This resilience is invaluable in a world where setbacks and changes are inevitable.

3. *Lifelong Learning:* With a growth mindset, you have an innate thirst for knowledge and development. This drives you to seek out opportunities for continuous learning and skill enhancement, which are essential in a rapidly changing job market.

4. *Embracing Change:* Change is a constant in today's work landscape. A growth mindset equips you to embrace change and adapt swiftly. You view change as a chance to evolve, not as a threat to your comfort zone.

5. *Building Resilience:* A growth mindset fosters emotional resilience. You're less likely to be discouraged by criticism or setbacks because you understand they're part of the growth process. This emotional resilience is a valuable asset in any career.

6. *Innovating and Problem-Solving:* Innovative thinking and creative problem-solving are byproducts of a growth mindset. You're open to exploring new ideas and uncharted territories, leading to breakthroughs in your career.

Strategies for Cultivating a Growth Mindset:

1. *Self-Awareness*: Start by recognizing when you have a fixed mindset. Be mindful of the voice in your head that says, "I can't do this" or "I'm not good at that." Challenge those thoughts and replace them with, "I can learn this" or "I haven't mastered this yet."
2. *Embrace Challenges:* Seek out challenges that push you beyond your comfort zone. Whether it's taking on a new project or learning a skill outside your expertise, relish the opportunity for growth.
3. *Learn from Failures:* When you encounter setbacks or failures, analyze them objectively. What can you learn from the experience? How can you apply these lessons in the future?
4. *Seek Feedback:* Welcome feedback, even if it's critical. Use it as an opportunity to

improve and grow. Constructive feedback is
a valuable tool for development.

5. ***Practice Persistence:*** Cultivating a growth
mindset requires persistence. Stay
committed to your goals, even when the
going gets tough. Remember that the path
to mastery is often paved with challenges.

6. ***Encourage Others:*** Promote a growth
mindset in your workplace or among peers.
Encourage others to embrace challenges
and view failures as learning opportunities.
Creating a culture of growth mindset can be
mutually beneficial.

Chapter 3

Assessing Your Skills

Before you can future-proof your career, you need a clear understanding of your current skills and strengths. Skill assessment is the compass that guides your journey toward career resilience and adaptability. Here's why assessing your skills is crucial and how to go about it effectively:

1. Self-Awareness: Assessing your skills begins with self-awareness. It's about taking an honest look at your abilities, knowledge, and competencies. This self-awareness forms the foundation upon which you'll build your career resilience.

2. Identifying Core Competencies: Start by identifying your core competencies—the skills and strengths that define your professional identity. These might be technical skills, such as coding or data analysis, or soft skills like leadership and communication.

3. Recognizing Transferable Skills: In addition to your core competencies, recognize your transferable skills. These are skills that can be applied across various roles and industries. Examples include problem-solving, project management, and adaptability.

4. Skill Gaps: Assessing your skills also involves identifying gaps. What skills are in high demand in your field or desired career path? What do you need to learn or improve to stay competitive?

5. Goal Alignment: Once you understand your skills, align them with your career goals. Are there skills you need to develop to achieve your objectives? Are there skills that no longer serve your goals and can be deprioritized?

6. Personalized Development Plan: Skill assessment leads to the creation of a personalized development plan. This plan outlines your goals for skill improvement, how you'll acquire these skills, and a timeline for achieving them.

7. Adaptability: By regularly assessing your skills, you become more adaptable. You can pivot when needed, acquiring new skills to meet evolving demands in your industry or profession.

Strategies for Skill Assessment:

1. *Self-Reflection*: Spend time reflecting on your past experiences, projects, and roles. What skills did you excel in? Where did you face challenges? This can reveal your strengths and areas for improvement.
2. *Feedback*: Seek feedback from peers, mentors, or supervisors. Others may provide valuable insights into your strengths and weaknesses that you might not see yourself.
3. *Self-Assessment Tools:* There are various self-assessment tools and tests available that can help you identify your strengths and areas for development. These can

provide a structured way to evaluate your skills.

4. *Industry Research:* Stay informed about industry trends and the skills in demand. Look at job postings and descriptions to identify the skills employers are seeking.

5. *Networking*: Engage with professionals in your field or desired career path. Conversations with others can provide insights into the skills that are most valuable in your industry.

6. *Online Courses and Training*: Enroll in online courses, workshops, or training programs to develop new skills or enhance existing ones. Many platforms offer courses on a wide range of topics.

7. *Mentorship*: Seek mentorship from individuals who have expertise in areas you wish to develop. Mentors can provide guidance and support as you work on your skills.

Identifying Strengths

Identifying your strengths is a foundational step in the journey of self-discovery and career development. Your strengths are the unique talents, abilities, and attributes that set you apart and can become powerful assets in your professional life. Here's why identifying your strengths is essential and how to go about it effectively:

1. Self-Understanding: Identifying your strengths begins with a deep understanding of yourself. It's about recognizing your natural abilities and the qualities that make you shine. This self-awareness is invaluable for making informed career choices.

2. Personal Branding: Your strengths are a core element of your personal brand. They communicate what you bring to the table and how you can contribute to an organization or industry. Knowing your strengths helps you market yourself effectively.

3. Career Alignment: Understanding your strengths allows you to align your career with your innate talents. When your work aligns with your strengths, you're more likely to excel, find fulfillment, and enjoy long-term success.

4. Confidence Boost: Recognizing your strengths boosts your confidence. When you're aware of what you do well, you approach challenges with a positive mindset, knowing you have the abilities to overcome them.

5. Skill Development: Identifying strengths can also highlight areas for skill development. You can focus on enhancing your strengths further or address complementary skills that can amplify your abilities.

Strategies for Identifying Strengths:

1. **Self-Reflection**: Spend time reflecting on your past experiences, achievements, and moments of flow. What tasks or activities came naturally to you? What did you enjoy doing without feeling drained?

2. ***Feedback from Others:*** Ask colleagues, friends, and mentors for their perspectives on your strengths. They may offer insights that you haven't considered.

3. ***Strengths Assessment*** Tools: Utilize strengths assessment tools like the CliftonStrengths or VIA Character Strengths survey. These assessments can provide structured insights into your strengths.

4. ***Keep a Strengths Journal:*** Document instances where you felt strong and capable in your work. Over time, patterns may emerge, revealing your dominant strengths.

5. ***Explore Diverse Experiences:*** Step out of your comfort zone and explore new experiences. You may discover hidden strengths in unfamiliar contexts.

6. ***Set SMART Goals:*** Define specific, measurable, achievable, relevant, and time-bound (SMART) goals that align with your strengths. Working toward these goals can highlight your abilities.

7. ***Seek Career Guidance:*** Consult with career counselors or coaches who specialize in

helping individuals identify and leverage their strengths.

8. ***Use Strengths in Projects***: In your current role or personal projects, actively seek opportunities to apply your strengths. This practical experience can reinforce your understanding of your abilities.

9. ***Peer Networking:*** Engage in professional networks or groups where you can collaborate with others who share similar strengths. Learning from others can enhance your self-awareness.

Chapter 4

Building Your Toolkit

In the ever-changing landscape of work, building and maintaining a versatile toolkit of skills is akin to equipping yourself with a Swiss Army knife for your career. Your toolkit represents a collection of competencies, both technical and soft, that enhance your adaptability, problem-solving abilities, and overall career resilience. Here's why building your toolkit is crucial and how to go about it effectively:

1. Adaptability and Agility: A diverse set of skills makes you adaptable and agile in the face of change. As industries evolve and job roles shift, your toolkit empowers you to pivot, take on new challenges, and seize emerging opportunities.

2. Career Flexibility: Building your toolkit enhances your career flexibility. It means you're not locked into a single job role or industry; you have the skills to transition to different roles or sectors when needed.

3. Problem-Solving Capability: A well-rounded toolkit equips you with problem-solving capabilities. You can approach complex issues from multiple angles, drawing on various skills to find innovative solutions.

4. Career Advancement: Many employers value employees with a broad skill set. Building your toolkit can open doors to new career opportunities, promotions, and increased earning potential.

5. Lifelong Learning: A commitment to building your toolkit is a commitment to lifelong learning. It encourages you to stay curious, seek out new knowledge, and continuously improve your skills.

Strategies for Building Your Toolkit:

1. **Identify Core Competencies**: Begin by identifying the core competencies relevant to your field or desired career path. These

might include technical skills (e.g., programming, data analysis) and soft skills (e.g., communication, leadership).

2. ***Assess Skill Gaps:*** Identify the skills you currently lack but are essential for your career goals. This helps you prioritize which skills to acquire.

3. ***Set Skill Development Goals***: Create specific skill development goals. Define what you want to achieve and establish a timeline for acquiring each skill.

4. ***Diverse Learning Resources:*** Utilize a variety of learning resources. This may include online courses, workshops, textbooks, mentors, and practical hands-on experience.

5. ***Practice and Application:*** Apply what you learn in real-world situations. Practical experience is often the most effective way to solidify your skills.

6. ***Continuous Learning:*** Make learning a habit. Dedicate time regularly to acquire new skills or deepen existing ones.

7. **Seek Feedback:** Request feedback from mentors, peers, or supervisors as you develop your skills. Constructive feedback can accelerate your growth.
8. **Networking and Collaboration**: Collaborate with professionals who possess complementary skills. Working on projects together can enhance your skill set and provide valuable experience.
9. **Certifications and Credentials:** Depending on your field, consider obtaining certifications or credentials that validate your skills and expertise.
10. **Stay Informed:** Keep up with industry trends, emerging technologies, and changes in best practices. Staying informed ensures that your skills remain relevant.

Skill Development and Lifelong Learning

In the dynamic landscape of the 21st century, the adage "knowledge is power" has evolved into "continuous learning is power." Skill development and lifelong learning have become not just valuable assets but essential lifelines to career resilience. Here's why these pursuits are pivotal and how to approach them effectively:

1. *Adapting to Change:* The pace of change in technology and industries is relentless. To stay relevant and adaptable, you must continuously acquire new skills and knowledge. Skill development and lifelong learning empower you to navigate change with confidence.

2. *Future-Proofing Your Career:* By honing existing skills and acquiring new ones, you future-proof your career. You're better equipped to thrive in an ever-evolving job market, where certain skills become obsolete while others gain prominence.

3. *Enhancing Problem-Solving Abilities:* Learning new skills and gaining knowledge enhances your problem-solving abilities. You're better equipped to address complex challenges and find innovative solutions, which is a valuable asset in any profession.

4. *Expanding Career Opportunities*: A commitment to skill development and lifelong learning expands your career horizons. You become eligible for a wider range of job opportunities, promotions, and career shifts.

5. *Staying Competitive:* In a competitive job market, continuous learning sets you apart. Employers value individuals who demonstrate a commitment to self-improvement and skill development.

Strategies for Skill Development and Lifelong Learning:

1. ***Identify Learning Goals:*** Define your learning objectives. What skills do you want to develop, and why? Set clear goals to guide your efforts.
2. ***Create a Learning Plan:*** Develop a structured plan for acquiring skills and

knowledge. Include a timeline, learning resources, and milestones to track progress.

3. ***Diverse Learning Sources:*** Utilize a variety of learning sources, including online courses, workshops, books, podcasts, webinars, and mentors. Mix formal education with practical experience.

4. ***Allocate Time Regularly:*** Dedicate time regularly to learning. Consistency is key to making meaningful progress.

5. ***Practice and Application:*** Apply what you learn in real-world scenarios. Practical experience reinforces your learning.

6. ***Seek Feedback***: Request feedback from mentors, peers, or instructors. Feedback helps you refine your skills and identify areas for improvement.

7. ***Networking***: Engage with professionals in your field or area of interest. Networking can provide valuable insights and learning opportunities.

8. ***Stay Informed:*** Stay abreast of industry trends and emerging technologies.

Subscribe to relevant publications and follow thought leaders in your field.

9. ***Online Learning Platforms***: Explore online learning platforms that offer a wide range of courses and resources, such as Coursera, edX, Udemy, and LinkedIn Learning.

10. ***Certifications and Credentials***: Consider obtaining certifications or credentials that validate your expertise in specific areas. These can enhance your credibility and career prospects.

11. ***Mentorship***: Seek mentorship from individuals who have expertise in the skills you're developing. Mentors can provide guidance and support on your learning journey.

12. ***Join Professional Associations***: Many industries have professional associations that offer educational resources and networking opportunities. Consider joining one related to your career.

Chapter 5

Creating a Resilience Plan

In an era defined by unpredictability and rapid change, the importance of a resilience plan cannot be overstated. This plan is your roadmap for navigating the uncertainties of life and career with grace and determination. Here's how to create a resilience plan that empowers you to not only weather storms but emerge stronger from them.

1. **Self-Assessment:** Start by taking stock of your strengths, weaknesses, and values. Understand your core competencies and areas for improvement. This self-awareness forms the foundation of your plan.

2. **Define Your Goals:** Clearly articulate your personal and professional goals. What do you want to achieve in the short term and long term? Your goals provide direction for your resilience plan.

3. *Identify Stressors*: Recognize the stressors and challenges that you may encounter on your journey. These could be career setbacks, health issues, or personal crises. Awareness allows you to prepare.

4. *Building a Support Network*: Cultivate a strong support network of friends, family, mentors, and colleagues. In times of adversity, they can provide emotional support and guidance.

5. *Skill Development:* Continuously develop and update your skills. A diverse skill set enhances your adaptability and problem-solving capabilities.

6. *Financial Preparedness:* Establish financial stability and savings to weather unexpected setbacks. Financial resilience is a pillar of overall resilience.

7. *Flexibility and Adaptability:* Embrace change as an opportunity for growth. Develop flexibility and adaptability as core traits to navigate uncertain terrain.

8. *Mindfulness and Well-being*: Prioritize mental and physical well-being. Practices like mindfulness and self-care enhance your emotional resilience.

9. *Crisis Response:* Develop a plan for how you'll respond to crises. Having a step-by-step approach can mitigate the impact of unexpected events.

10. *Learn from Setbacks*: Embrace setbacks as learning opportunities. Analyze what went wrong, what you've learned, and how you can apply those lessons moving forward.

11. *Positive Mindset:* Cultivate a positive mindset. Optimism and resilience go hand in hand; they fuel your ability to bounce back from adversity.

Setting Clear Goals

Setting clear goals is the compass that directs your journey toward success. It's the process of defining specific objectives and outlining the steps needed to reach them. Clear goals provide focus, motivation, and a sense of purpose. Whether in your personal life or career, having well-defined goals empowers you to:

1. *Prioritize*: Clear goals help you identify what's most important. They allow you to allocate your time and resources to the tasks that align with your objectives.

2. *Measure Progress:* When your goals are clear, you can track your progress effectively. This measurement provides a sense of accomplishment and helps you stay on course.

3. *Stay Motivated:* Goals act as powerful motivators. They give you a reason to persevere, even when faced with challenges or setbacks.

4. *Make Informed Decisions:* With clear goals, decision-making becomes more straightforward. You can evaluate choices based on whether they align with your objectives.

5. *Achieve Success*: Clarity in your goals sets the stage for success. It provides a roadmap that

guides your efforts and maximizes your chances of reaching your desired outcomes.

Whether you're aiming for personal growth, career advancement, or any other aspiration, setting clear and actionable goals is the first step towards turning your dreams into reality.

Chapter 6

Thriving at Work

Thriving at work goes beyond merely clocking in and fulfilling your job responsibilities. It's about finding fulfillment, achieving your career goals, and contributing meaningfully to your organization. In the modern workplace, where change is constant and competition is fierce, thriving is an aspiration worth pursuing. Here are strategies to help you thrive at work:

1. Define Your Purpose: Start by understanding your personal and professional values. What drives you? What are your long-term goals and aspirations? Knowing your purpose provides clarity and motivation.

2. Continuous Learning: Embrace a mindset of continuous learning. Invest in your skills and knowledge. Stay current with industry trends and technologies. This not only makes you more valuable to your employer but also boosts your confidence.

3. Goal Setting: Set clear and achievable goals. Whether they're daily, weekly, or long-term objectives, goals provide direction and a sense of accomplishment when achieved.

4. Time Management: Master time management. Prioritize tasks, set boundaries, and minimize distractions. Efficiently managing your time can reduce stress and increase productivity.

5. Networking: Build and nurture professional relationships. Networking can open doors to opportunities, provide support, and offer valuable insights into your industry.

6. Adaptability: Develop adaptability. The ability to embrace change, pivot when necessary, and thrive in evolving circumstances is essential in today's dynamic work environment.

7. Resilience: Cultivate resilience. You'll face challenges and setbacks, but it's how you bounce back from them that matters. Learn from failures and stay determined.

8. *Communication*: Effective communication is a cornerstone of thriving at work. Be clear, concise, and open in your interactions with colleagues and superiors.

9. *Work-Life Balance*: Maintain a healthy work-life balance. Prioritize self-care, family, and personal interests. A well-balanced life supports your overall well-being and performance at work.

10. *Embrace Leadership*: Even if you're not in a formal leadership role, embrace leadership qualities. Take initiative, inspire others, and lead by example. This not only benefits your career but also contributes to a positive workplace culture.

11. *Seek Feedback:* Welcome feedback from peers and supervisors. Constructive feedback is a powerful tool for growth and improvement.

12. Find Meaning: Connect your work to a sense of purpose. Understand how your contributions make a difference, and find meaning in your daily tasks.

13. Manage Stress: Develop effective stress management techniques. Exercise, mindfulness, and relaxation can help you handle workplace pressures.

14. Celebrate Achievements: Don't forget to celebrate your achievements, no matter how small. Acknowledging your successes reinforces your sense of accomplishment and motivates further success.

Thriving at work is not a one-size-fits-all journey. It's a personal and ongoing pursuit that involves continuous self-improvement and adaptation. By embracing these strategies, you can not only excel in your career but also find fulfilment and satisfaction in your professional life.

Strategies for Agility

In today's rapidly changing world, agility has become a crucial skill for individuals and organisations alike. Agility is the ability to adapt and respond swiftly and effectively to shifts in the environment, whether they're technological advancements, market fluctuations, or unexpected challenges. Here are strategies for cultivating agility:

1. Embrace a Growth Mindset: Develop a growth mindset, which sees challenges as opportunities for learning and growth. This mindset fosters adaptability and a willingness to experiment.

2. Continuous Learning: Prioritize continuous learning. Stay updated on industry trends, emerging technologies, and best practices. The more you know, the better prepared you are to adapt.

3. Flexibility in Decision-Making: Be open to changing your course of action when circumstances dictate. Flexibility in decision-making enables you to respond to new information or unexpected developments.

4. Cross-Functional Teams: Collaborate with colleagues from diverse backgrounds and expertise. Cross-functional teams bring together a range of perspectives and skills, promoting creative problem-solving.

5. Scenario Planning: Anticipate different scenarios and their potential impact. This foresight helps you prepare for various outcomes and make informed decisions.

6. Agile Methodologies: Explore agile methodologies like Scrum or Kanban, which are commonly used in project management. These frameworks promote flexibility, collaboration, and iterative progress.

7. Risk-Taking: Be willing to take calculated risks. Agility often involves venturing into uncharted territory. Learning from both successes and failures is part of the process.

8. Rapid Prototyping: Innovation often requires rapid prototyping and testing. This approach allows you to experiment with ideas and iterate quickly.

9. Data-Driven Decision-Making: Leverage data and analytics to inform your decisions. Data-driven insights provide a solid foundation for adapting to changing circumstances.

10. Leadership Buy-In: Cultivate a culture of agility within your organisation. Secure buy-in from leadership, as their support is essential for fostering an agile mindset throughout the company.

11. Resilience Building: Invest in building personal and organisational resilience. Resilience enables you to recover quickly from setbacks and continue moving forward.

12. Time Management:

Effectively manage your time and priorities. Clear priorities allow you to respond to changing demands more efficiently.

13. *Adaptability in Skills:* Stay adaptable in your skill set. Don't become overly specialized to the point where change is difficult. A broad skill base enhances your agility.

14. *Stay Informed*: Regularly consume information from various sources. Staying informed about global events, industry trends, and emerging technologies keeps you ahead of the curve.

15. *Feedback Loop:* Establish a feedback loop for continuous improvement. Encourage candid feedback from colleagues and peers to refine your approaches.

Chapter 7

Entrepreneurial Thinking

Entrepreneurial thinking is a mindset that extends far beyond starting a business. It's a way of approaching challenges, opportunities, and the world itself with a unique blend of creativity, innovation, and a willingness to take calculated risks. This mindset has become increasingly valuable in various aspects of life, from corporate environments to personal pursuits. Here's what entrepreneurial thinking entails and why it matters:

1. Problem-Solving Focus: Entrepreneurial thinkers view problems as opportunities. Instead of avoiding challenges, they actively seek solutions, often turning problems into innovative ventures or improvements.

2. Creativity and Innovation: At the heart of entrepreneurial thinking is creativity. Entrepreneurs are known for thinking outside the box, imagining new products, services, and ways of doing things that others might not have considered.

3. Risk-Taking: While entrepreneurs take risks, they are calculated ones. They weigh potential rewards against risks and are not deterred by the possibility of failure. Risk-taking is seen as a path to learning and growth.

4. Adaptability: Entrepreneurial thinkers are adaptable and thrive in rapidly changing environments. They can pivot their strategies and approaches as circumstances evolve.

5. Initiative: Entrepreneurs take initiative. They don't wait for permission or for someone else to solve problems. They proactively identify opportunities and take action.

6. Resilience: Resilience is a hallmark of entrepreneurial thinking. Even in the face of failure or setbacks, entrepreneurs bounce back, learn from their experiences, and continue forward.

7. *Vision:* Entrepreneurial thinkers have a clear vision of what they want to achieve. They set ambitious goals and work relentlessly toward them, often with a long-term perspective.

8. *Resourcefulness:* Entrepreneurs are resourceful, making the most of available resources and seeking creative solutions to challenges, whether it's financial constraints or limited time.

9. *Networking:* Entrepreneurial thinkers understand the value of building a strong network. They cultivate relationships with mentors, collaborators, and peers who can provide guidance and support.

10. *Learning Orientation:* Entrepreneurial thinking is marked by a continuous learning orientation. Entrepreneurs are curious and open to acquiring new knowledge and skills.

11. *Customer-Centric Approach:*

Entrepreneurs prioritize understanding and meeting customer needs. They are driven by the desire to create products or services that provide value and address real-world problems.

12. Positive Mindset: Entrepreneurial thinkers maintain a positive and optimistic outlook. They view challenges as opportunities for growth and maintain a "can-do" attitude.

13. Ethical Considerations: Ethical considerations are paramount in entrepreneurial thinking. Entrepreneurs strive to create businesses and solutions that align with ethical principles and societal values.

Exploring New Opportunities

Exploring new opportunities is a dynamic and essential aspect of personal and professional development. Whether you're seeking career advancement, embarking on an entrepreneurial venture, or simply looking for fresh experiences, the pursuit of new opportunities is a powerful driver of growth and success. Here's why it matters and how to approach it effectively:

1. Catalyst for Growth: Exploring new opportunities challenges you to step outside your comfort zone. It's in these uncharted territories that personal and professional growth often occurs.

2. Broadening Horizons: New opportunities introduce you to diverse perspectives, people, and environments. This broadens your horizons, enriching your life and expanding your knowledge.

3. Overcoming Fear: The fear of the unknown can be paralyzing, but exploring new opportunities allows you to confront and conquer this fear. With each step into the unknown, you become more resilient and adaptable.

4. Building Resilience: Navigating new opportunities often involves overcoming obstacles and setbacks. These experiences build emotional and mental resilience, essential qualities for success.

5. Innovation and Creativity: New opportunities stimulate your creativity and encourage innovative thinking. They inspire fresh ideas and approaches to problem-solving.

6. Career Advancement: In your professional life, exploring new opportunities can lead to career advancement, increased earning potential, and personal fulfilment.

7. Entrepreneurship: For entrepreneurs, the exploration of new opportunities is the foundation of innovation and business growth. It's about identifying unmet needs and creating solutions.

Strategies for Exploring New Opportunities:

1. **Self-Reflection:** Begin by identifying your goals, passions, and areas of interest. What opportunities align with your values and aspirations?
2. **Networking:** Connect with professionals, mentors, and peers who can provide insights and introductions to new opportunities.

3. **Stay Informed**: Continuously educate yourself about industry trends, emerging technologies, and market developments. This knowledge can reveal potential opportunities.

4. **Take Calculated Risks**: While exploring new opportunities involves risks, they should be calculated. Evaluate potential risks and rewards before taking action.

5. **Learn from Failure:** Don't fear failure; embrace it as a valuable teacher. Analyze what went wrong, extract lessons, and apply them to future opportunities.

6. **Set Clear Goals:** Define specific, achievable goals for each opportunity you pursue. Goals provide direction and measurement of success.

7. **Time Management:** Manage your time effectively to balance exploring new opportunities with existing commitments.

8. **Experiment and Iterate:** Be open to experimentation. Not all opportunities will lead to the desired outcome, but each can inform your path forward.

9. *Embrace Change*: Be adaptable and willing
    to pivot when necessary. The ability to
    adapt is key to capitalizing on new
    opportunities.
10. *Seek Feedback*: Solicit feedback from
    trusted individuals. They can provide
    valuable insights and help you refine your
    approach.

Chapter 8

Technology for Advancement

Technology has emerged as a powerful catalyst for advancement, revolutionizing industries, improving quality of life, and shaping the future in profound ways. It's a driving force behind economic growth, innovation, and societal development. Here's how technology fuels advancement and why it's pivotal in our modern world:

1. Driving Innovation: Technology fosters innovation by enabling individuals and organizations to conceive, develop, and implement novel ideas and solutions. It provides the tools and platforms for creative thinking and problem-solving.

2. Economic Growth: Technological advancements drive economic growth. Industries that embrace technology tend to experience increased productivity, job creation, and competitive advantages on a global scale.

3. *Access to Information:* The internet and digital technologies have democratised access to information. They empower people to learn, collaborate, and share knowledge regardless of geographical or socioeconomic barriers.

4. *Healthcare Breakthroughs*: In healthcare, technology has led to significant breakthroughs in diagnostics, treatment, and patient care. It extends life expectancy, improves disease management, and enhances overall well-being.

5. *Environmental Sustainability:* Technology plays a critical role in addressing environmental challenges. Innovations like renewable energy, smart grids, and sustainable agriculture contribute to a more eco-friendly and sustainable future.

6. ***Connectivity***: Technological advancements in communication and connectivity have brought the

world closer together. They facilitate global collaboration, trade, and cultural exchange.

7. *Automation and Efficiency*: Automation technologies, including robotics and artificial intelligence, streamline processes and improve efficiency across various sectors, from manufacturing to logistics.

8. *Personalization:* Technology allows for personalized experiences and products. This customization enhances user satisfaction and meets individual needs more effectively.

9. *Data Analytics:* Big data analytics harness vast amounts of data to derive insights and inform decision-making. This data-driven approach fuels progress in diverse fields, from marketing to healthcare.

10. *Education and Lifelong Learning:* Digital learning platforms and educational technologies make education more accessible and adaptable.

They promote lifelong learning and skill development.

11. Disaster Response: Technology aids in disaster response and recovery efforts. Innovations in remote sensing, predictive analytics, and communication systems enhance preparedness and resilience.

12. Empowering Entrepreneurs: Technology lowers barriers to entrepreneurship. It enables startups and small businesses to access markets, resources, and customers globally.

13. Space Exploration: Technological advancements drive space exploration, expanding our understanding of the universe and paving the way for potential future colonisation.

14. Access to Financial Services: Financial technologies (FinTech) increase access to banking and financial services, particularly in underserved regions.

15. Assistive Technologies: Technology enhances the quality of life for individuals with disabilities through assistive devices and accessibility features in software and hardware.

16. Smart Cities: The concept of smart cities leverages technology to optimize infrastructure, transportation, energy consumption, and public services for urban populations

Leveraging Digital Tools

In our increasingly digital world, the effective use of digital tools has become a cornerstone of personal and professional success. These tools encompass a wide range of software, apps, and online platforms designed to enhance productivity, communication, and problem-solving. Here's why leveraging digital tools is pivotal and how to harness their potential effectively:

1. Efficiency and Productivity: Digital tools streamline tasks, automate processes, and boost efficiency. They help you complete work more

quickly and accurately, leaving you with more time
to focus on high-impact activities.

2. Collaboration and Communication: Digital tools
facilitate seamless collaboration and
communication, especially in remote or distributed
work environments. They enable real-time
interactions, file sharing, and project management.

3. Data Management: Organizing and managing
data is simplified with digital tools. From cloud
storage to database software, these tools help you
access, analyze, and safeguard data effectively.

4. Accessibility: Digital tools are often accessible
from anywhere with an internet connection. This
accessibility allows for flexibility in work
arrangements and ensures you can stay connected
on the go.

5. Decision-Making Support: Analytics and data
visualization tools provide valuable insights to
inform decision-making. They help you make

data-driven choices in various aspects of life and business.

6. *Learning and Skill Development:* Online learning platforms and educational apps facilitate lifelong learning and skill development. You can acquire new knowledge and competencies at your own pace.

7. *Creativity and Innovation:* Digital tools enhance creativity through graphic design software, creative writing apps, and multimedia production tools. They empower you to bring ideas to life.

8. *Personal Organization:* Digital calendars, task managers, and note-taking apps keep your personal and professional life organized. They help you set goals and track progress.

9. *Financial Management:* Financial apps assist with budgeting, investing, and expense tracking. They provide a comprehensive view of your financial health and enable smarter financial decisions.

10. Marketing and Promotion: Digital marketing tools, such as social media management platforms and email marketing software, help businesses reach and engage their target audience.

11. Health and Wellness: Wellness apps and wearable devices monitor health metrics and encourage healthy habits. They promote physical and mental well-being.

12. Project Management: Project management software streamlines project planning, task delegation, and progress tracking. It enhances collaboration among team members.

Strategies for Leveraging Digital Tools:

1. **Assess Needs:** Identify your specific needs and objectives before choosing digital tools. Determine whether a tool aligns with your goals.
2. **Learn and Master:** Invest time in learning how to use digital tools effectively. Many

offer tutorials and user communities for support.

3. **Integrate Tools:** Integrate tools into your daily routines and workflows. Make them an integral part of how you work and communicate.

4. **Stay Updated:** Technology evolves rapidly. Regularly update your knowledge of existing tools and explore new ones to stay current.

5. **Customize and Personalize:** Tailor digital tools to your preferences and needs. Adjust settings and features to optimize their utility.

6. **Data Security**: Be vigilant about data security and privacy. Use secure passwords, enable two-factor authentication, and understand data sharing settings.

7. **Feedback and Evaluation**: Seek feedback from colleagues or peers who use similar tools. Periodically evaluate whether a tool continues to meet your needs.

8. **Minimize Tool Overload:** Avoid the temptation to use too many tools

simultaneously. Simplify your toolkit to
focus on essentials.

Chapter 9

Overcoming Challenges

Life is filled with challenges, and the journey to success is often accompanied by hurdles, setbacks, and adversity. Yet, it's in facing and overcoming these challenges that personal growth, resilience, and achievement are nurtured. Here's how to navigate obstacles effectively and emerge stronger on the other side:

1. Resilience Building: Resilience is the ability to bounce back from adversity. Cultivate this trait by viewing challenges as opportunities for growth. Each obstacle you overcome adds to your resilience.

2. Positive Mindset: Maintain a positive mindset. A positive attitude not only helps you persevere through challenges but also enables creative problem-solving.

3. Problem-Solving Skills: Develop strong problem-solving skills. Break complex challenges into smaller, manageable steps and seek practical solutions.

4. Adaptability: Embrace change and adaptability as constants in life. Being flexible in your approach allows you to pivot when necessary and navigate shifting circumstances.

5. Support Network: Lean on your support network. Friends, family, mentors, and colleagues can provide guidance, encouragement, and emotional support during tough times.

6. Goal Setting: Set clear, achievable goals. Goals provide direction and motivation, even when facing difficulties.

7. Learn from Failure: Failure is often a stepping stone to success. Analyze what went wrong, extract valuable lessons, and apply them in future endeavors.

8. *Self-Care:* Prioritize self-care. A well-rested and healthy mind and body are better equipped to handle challenges.

9. *Time Management:* Effective time management helps you allocate resources to tackle challenges while balancing other responsibilities.

10. *Seek Perspective:* Gain perspective by looking at the bigger picture. Consider how the challenge fits into your overall journey and long-term goals.

11. *Seek Guidance:* Don't hesitate to seek guidance or expertise when needed. Consulting experts or mentors can provide valuable insights and solutions.

12. *Break Tasks Down:* When facing a daunting challenge, break it down into smaller, manageable tasks. This makes the challenge feel less overwhelming.

13. *Embrace Patience:* Understand that overcoming challenges may take time. Be patient with yourself and the process.

14. *Self-Reflection:* Reflect on your values and priorities. Challenges can prompt you to reassess and align your actions with your core beliefs.

15. *Celebrate Progress:* Acknowledge and celebrate your progress, no matter how small. Recognizing your achievements boosts motivation.

16. *Perseverance:* Above all, persevere. Challenges may test your determination, but the act of persevering is a powerful testament to your resolve.

17. *Embrace Change*: Sometimes, challenges force us to change course or rethink our plans. Embrace these shifts as opportunities for personal and professional growth.

Challenges are an inherent part of life's journey. Instead of viewing them as roadblocks, see them as stepping stones to a stronger, wiser, and more resilient version of yourself.

Dealing with Setbacks

Setbacks are an inevitable part of life's journey. Whether in personal goals, career pursuits, or relationships, setbacks can be disheartening and frustrating. However, they also offer valuable lessons, opportunities for growth, and a chance to demonstrate resilience. Here's how to effectively deal with setbacks and emerge stronger:

1. Accept Emotions: It's natural to feel disappointment, frustration, or even sadness when faced with setbacks. Allow yourself to acknowledge and process these emotions rather than suppressing them.

2. Reframe Your Perspective: Try to reframe setbacks as opportunities for growth and learning. Instead of seeing them as failures, view them as stepping stones on the path to success.

3. Analyze the Situation: Take a step back and analyze what led to the setback. Identify the factors that contributed to it, whether they were within or beyond your control.

4. Set Realistic Expectations: Reflect on whether your expectations were realistic. Sometimes, setbacks occur because goals were overly ambitious or timelines were too tight.

5. Self-Compassion: Be kind to yourself. Avoid self-blame and negative self-talk. Treat yourself with the same compassion and encouragement you would offer a friend.

6. Seek Support: Lean on your support network. Friends, family, mentors, and colleagues can provide valuable guidance, perspective, and emotional support during challenging times.

7. Learn from the Experience: Consider what you can learn from the setback. What insights or skills can you gain from this experience? How can you avoid similar pitfalls in the future?

8. Adapt and Adjust: Use the lessons learned to adapt and adjust your approach. Modify your strategies or goals as needed to move forward effectively.

9. *Stay Persistent:* Persistence is key to overcoming setbacks. Don't give up on your goals or dreams. Keep moving forward, even if progress is slow.

10. *Visualize Success:* Visualize your future success. Maintain a clear image of your goals and the positive outcomes you aim to achieve. Visualization can boost motivation.

11. *Focus on What You Can Control*: Acknowledge that some aspects of setbacks may be beyond your control. Focus your energy on the elements you can influence and change.

12. *Seek Professional Help:* In some cases, setbacks may have a significant impact on your mental or emotional well-being. Don't hesitate to seek professional help if needed, such as counseling or therapy.

13. *Stay Resilient:* Cultivate resilience as a core trait. Resilience enables you to bounce back from setbacks with greater strength and determination.

14. Embrace Flexibility: Be open to adapting your goals and plans as circumstances evolve. Flexibility allows you to navigate unexpected challenges.

15. Keep a Growth Mindset: Maintain a growth mindset. Embrace challenges as opportunities for learning and personal development.

16. Celebrate Progress: Acknowledge and celebrate small victories along the way. These moments of success can boost your confidence and motivation.

17. Stay Persistent: Above all, persevere. Setbacks are part of any worthwhile journey. The ability to keep moving forward, even in the face of adversity, is a testament to your strength and determination.

Chapter 10

Success Stories

1. Career Transformation - *Meet Sarah:*

Sarah had spent years in a corporate job that paid the bills but left her unfulfilled. She felt a deep passion for photography, but the fear of leaving her stable job held her back. this book served as a catalyst for her transformation. Inspired by the chapters on pursuing one's passion and embracing change, Sarah decided to take the leap.

She started by taking photography classes, honing her skills, and building a portfolio. Networking became her second nature, and she connected with fellow photographers and potential clients through social media. Sarah's dedication paid off when she secured her first paid photography gig. Her client base grew steadily, thanks to her remarkable talent and relentless commitment.

Sarah's success story illustrates how applying the principles of embracing change, cultivating a growth mindset, and leveraging her passion led to a fulfilling career transformation. this book gave her the confidence to pursue her dreams, resulting in both personal fulfillment and financial success.

2. *Entrepreneurial Journey* - *The Story of Mark:*

Mark's entrepreneurial journey was a rollercoaster of highs and lows. He founded a tech startup based on an innovative idea but faced numerous setbacks along the way. After reading this book's chapters on resilience and adaptability, Mark was inspired to persevere.

He encountered funding challenges, product development setbacks, and even a market pivot. However, instead of giving up, he embraced each obstacle as a learning opportunity. He engaged with mentors, sought customer feedback, and fine-tuned his business model. Mark's resilience and unwavering belief in his vision eventually paid off when he secured a major round of funding.

Today, Mark's startup is a thriving company that's changing the industry. His journey is a testament to the principles of resilience, learning from failure, and staying committed to a vision, all of which were highlighted in this book.

3. Personal Growth and Well-Being - *Emily's Transformation:*

Emily's story is one of personal growth and well-being. She had reached a point of burnout in her demanding job, and her physical and mental health were suffering. this book's chapters on self-care and personal growth served as a lifeline.

Emily decided to prioritize her well-being by incorporating mindfulness practices into her daily routine. She also took your advice on time management to heart, allowing her to regain control over her schedule. Seeking support from a therapist provided her with the tools to manage stress and anxiety effectively.

Over time, Emily not only restored her health but also discovered a renewed sense of purpose. She began volunteering for a cause she deeply cared about, further enhancing her overall well-being. Emily's transformation exemplifies the principles of self-care, personal growth, and resilience advocated in this book.

4. Overcoming Obstacles - *From Adversity to Triumph:*

This success story focuses on an individual who faced significant adversity, such as health challenges, financial setbacks, and personal crises. Through the principles of resilience, determination, and learning from setbacks highlighted in this book, they were able to overcome obstacles that seemed insurmountable.

This story serves as a source of inspiration for readers grappling with their own challenges. It illustrates how, with the right mindset and strategies, individuals can navigate adversity and emerge stronger on the other side.

5. *Social Impact and Community Building* - *Jake's Impactful Initiative:*

Jake's story centers on his journey to create a nonprofit organization that addresses a pressing local issue. this book's chapters on community engagement, strategic planning, and social impact played a pivotal role in his success.

Jake's determination and strategic thinking led him to assemble a dedicated team of volunteers, secure funding, and establish partnerships with local businesses. Their collective efforts made a significant impact on the community, addressing the issue at its root.

Jake's story highlights the power of applying principles of community engagement, strategic planning, and social impact to drive positive change in the world. It inspires readers to consider how they can make a meaningful difference in their own communities.

6. *Financial Success and Wealth Building -* *Laura's Financial Journey:*

Laura's success story showcases her journey from financial instability to financial independence by applying the financial planning and investment strategies highlighted in this book.

After reading this book, Laura created a comprehensive financial plan that included budgeting, investing, and debt management. Over time, she built a diversified investment portfolio and made informed financial decisions that led to financial security and independence.

Laura's story is a practical guide for readers seeking to achieve their financial goals. It demonstrates how the principles of financial planning, disciplined saving, and informed investment can lead to financial success.

7. Leadership and Professional Advancement -
John's Leadership Rise:

John's journey from a mid-level manager to a high-impact leader is a story of effective leadership development. By implementing leadership principles from this book, he not only advanced his career but also fostered a culture of growth and innovation within his organization.

John embraced continuous learning, sought mentorship, and applied leadership strategies such as effective communication and team empowerment. His story illustrates how individuals can cultivate leadership skills and drive professional advancement while positively influencing their teams and organizations.

Real-Life Examples of Adaptation

Adaptation is a fundamental human trait that enables us to survive and thrive in an ever-changing world. Throughout history, individuals and societies have demonstrated remarkable adaptability in the face of challenges and transformations. Here are some compelling real-life examples of adaptation:

1. Darwin's Theory of Evolution:

Charles Darwin's theory of evolution by natural selection is a foundational example of adaptation in the natural world. He observed how species adapt to their environments over time, leading to the development of new traits that enhance their survival. This theory revolutionized our understanding of how life on Earth has evolved.

2. The Industrial Revolution: The Industrial Revolution, which began in the late 18th century, marked a dramatic shift in how societies organized production and labor. People adapted to new technologies and urbanization, transitioning from agrarian lifestyles to industrial ones. This transformation had profound economic, social, and cultural impacts across the globe.

3. *Digital Revolution:* The advent of the internet and digital technologies has brought about significant changes in the way we communicate, work, and live. Individuals and businesses have adapted to these innovations, leading to the rise of the digital age. This ongoing transformation has reshaped industries, created new opportunities, and changed the way we access information and connect with one another.

4. *Pandemic Response:* The COVID-19 pandemic forced individuals, governments, and healthcare systems to adapt rapidly to an unprecedented global crisis. People around the world adopted new behaviors, such as mask-wearing and social distancing, to reduce the virus's spread. Healthcare professionals adapted their treatment protocols, and researchers worked tirelessly to develop vaccines in record time.

5. *Space Exploration:* Exploration beyond Earth requires continuous adaptation to extreme conditions. Astronauts adapt to microgravity, radiation, and isolation during space missions.

Engineers and scientists develop cutting-edge technologies to support space travel, from life support systems to space habitats. This adaptation enables humans to explore and expand into space.

6. *Wildlife Conservation:* In the face of habitat loss and climate change, wildlife species have had to adapt to new conditions or face extinction. Some animals have altered their behavior, migration patterns, or diets to survive in changing environments. Conservationists work to protect and preserve these species by implementing adaptive management strategies.

7. *Sustainable Agriculture:* Agriculture faces the challenge of feeding a growing global population while minimizing environmental impact. Farmers are adapting by implementing sustainable farming practices, such as crop rotation, precision agriculture, and organic farming, to conserve resources and reduce the ecological footprint of agriculture.

8. *Cultural Adaptation:* Cultural adaptation occurs when individuals or communities adopt new customs, languages, or traditions due to migration or exposure to different cultures. This process can lead to cultural enrichment and the blending of diverse traditions. Examples include the cultural adaptation of immigrants in a new country and the globalization of cuisine and fashion.

9. *Climate Change Resilience*: Communities in vulnerable regions are adapting to the effects of climate change, such as rising sea levels and extreme weather events. Adaptation strategies may include building resilient infrastructure, implementing disaster preparedness plans, and transitioning to renewable energy sources.

10. *Business Innovation:* Businesses must adapt to changing market dynamics and consumer preferences. Companies like Amazon have successfully adapted by evolving from an online bookstore into a global e-commerce and technology giant. This adaptability has allowed them to thrive in a rapidly changing retail landscape.

These real-life examples illustrate the diverse ways in which individuals, societies, and ecosystems adapt to change and uncertainty.

Conclusion

Embracing Change and Crafting Your Future

In the pages of this book, we've embarked on a journey of transformation, resilience, and personal growth. We've explored the essential skills and mindsets needed to navigate an ever-changing world, adapt to challenges, and craft a future filled with purpose and success.

Through the inspiring stories of individuals who have triumphed over adversity, we've witnessed the incredible power of human adaptability. We've seen how determination, creativity, and an unwavering commitment to growth can lead to remarkable achievements.

We've delved into the importance of embracing change, understanding future trends, and cultivating a growth mindset. We've learned how to assess our skills, identify strengths, and build a toolkit that equips us for the challenges and opportunities that lie ahead.

Throughout these pages, we've discovered the value of lifelong learning and skill development, recognizing that our journey towards success is an ongoing evolution.

We've explored the art of resilience, learning how to bounce back from setbacks, face obstacles head-on, and emerge stronger than ever before.

We've explored the significance of setting clear goals, creating resilience plans, and thriving in our careers. We've examined strategies for agility and entrepreneurial thinking, and we've seen how technology can be harnessed to advance our endeavors.

As we conclude this book, remember that your journey doesn't end here—it's just beginning. You hold within you the potential to adapt, grow, and create a future filled with purpose and fulfillment.

The world will continue to change, and challenges will arise, but armed with the knowledge and insights gained from these pages, you are better prepared than ever to navigate the twists and turns of life's path.

So, step boldly into the future, armed with resilience, a growth mindset, and a toolkit of skills. Embrace change as an opportunity, set your goals high, and remember that success is not a destination but a continuous journey.

Your Personal Action Plan: Turning Knowledge into Results

As you reach the end of this book, you've gained valuable insights, strategies, and inspiration for navigating change, adapting to challenges, and crafting a successful future. Now, it's time to transform this knowledge into action through a personalized plan. Here's how to create your own action plan:

1. *Self-Reflection:* Begin by reflecting on your goals, values, and aspirations. What do you want to achieve in your career, personal life, or any other area that matters to you? Be clear about your objectives, both short-term and long-term.

2. *Identify Areas of Focus:* Based on what you've learned from this book, identify specific areas where you'd like to apply the principles of adaptation, growth, and resilience. Is it in your career, personal development, relationships, or a combination of these?

3. *Set Clear Goals:* Define clear and measurable goals for each area of focus. Your goals should be specific, achievable, and time-bound. For example, if your focus is on career advancement, your goal could be to secure a promotion within the next 12 months.

4. *Break Goals into Actionable Steps*: Divide your goals into smaller, actionable steps. These steps should outline the specific actions you need to take to move closer to your objectives. Each step should be manageable and achievable.

5. *Create a Timeline:* Assign deadlines to your goals and action steps. A timeline will help you stay accountable and track your progress. Make sure your timeline is realistic and allows for necessary adjustments.

6. *Prioritize and Focus:* Not all goals and actions are equally important. Prioritize your objectives based on their significance and urgency. Focus your energy and resources on what matters most to you.

7. *Build a Support System:* Share your goals and action plan with trusted friends, family members, or mentors. Having a support system can provide encouragement, guidance, and accountability.

8. *Embrace Lifelong Learning:* Commit to ongoing learning and skill development. Identify courses, workshops, or resources that will help you acquire new knowledge and improve your capabilities.

9. *Cultivate Resilience:* Understand that setbacks are a natural part of any journey. Develop a resilient mindset that allows you to bounce back from challenges with determination and adaptability.

10. *Monitor Progress:* Regularly review your action plan and track your progress. Celebrate your achievements, no matter how small, and make adjustments if needed.

11. *Stay Flexible:* Be open to adjusting your plan as circumstances change. Adaptability is a key factor in achieving long-term success.

12. *Seek Feedback:* Ask for feedback from trusted individuals who can provide insights and suggestions. Feedback can help you refine your approach and stay on the right track.

13. *Take Action:* The most crucial step is taking action. Your plan is a roadmap, but you must actively follow it to achieve your goals. Consistent action is the key to turning your aspirations into reality.

Remember that your personal action plan is a dynamic document that can evolve as you grow and your circumstances change. The principles you've learned in this book—embrace change, cultivate resilience, and foster a growth mindset—will serve as your guiding philosophy on your journey to success.

As you close this book, let it be a reminder that you have the power to shape your destiny, adapt to any circumstance, and create a future that reflects your deepest aspirations. Your story is still being written, and it holds the potential for greatness. So, go forth with confidence, and may your journey be filled with success, purpose, and the joy of continual growth.

Appendix

In this appendix, you'll find a curated list of resources to further support your journey of adaptation, personal growth, and success. These resources encompass books, websites, courses, and tools that can enhance your understanding and application of the principles discussed in this book.

Books:

1. *"Mindset: The New Psychology of Success" by Carol S. Dweck* - Explores the concept of a growth mindset and its impact on personal and professional development.
2. *"Grit: The Power of Passion and Perseverance" by Angela Duckworth* - Examines the role of grit and determination in achieving long-term goals.

3. *"The Lean Startup" by Eric Ries* - Offers insights into entrepreneurial thinking, lean methodologies, and innovation in business.
4. *"Atomic Habits" by James Clear* - Provides practical guidance on building and sustaining positive habits that lead to personal and professional success.
5. *"The Resilience Factor" by Karen Reivich and Andrew Shatte* - Delves into the science of resilience and provides strategies for enhancing this crucial trait.

Websites and Online Resources:

1. *Coursera (coursera.org)* - Offers a wide range of online courses, including those related to leadership, personal development, and career advancement.
2. *TED Talks (ted.com)* - Provides a wealth of inspiring talks on various topics, including resilience, innovation, and personal growth.

3. *LinkedIn Learning (linkedin.com/learning) -*
   Features courses on professional
   development, leadership, and adaptability in
   the workplace.
4. *Mindful (mindful.org)* - Offers resources and
   articles on mindfulness practices and stress
   reduction techniques.
5. *Harvard Business Review (hbr.org) -*
   Publishes articles and research on
   leadership, management, and workplace
   dynamics.

Tools and Apps:

1. *Todoist (todoist.com)* - A task management
   app that helps you organize your goals and
   action steps.
2. *Evernote (evernote.com)* - A note-taking and
   organization app to capture ideas and
   insights.

3. *Headspace (headspace.com)* - A meditation and mindfulness app for stress reduction and mental clarity.
4. *Trello (trello.com)* - A project management tool for visualizing and tracking your goals and action steps.
5. *Duolingo (duolingo.com)* - A language-learning app that fosters continuous learning and skill development.

Professional Organizations and Networking:

1. *Toastmasters International (toastmasters.org)* - A global organization that helps individuals improve their public speaking and leadership skills.
2. *Meetup (meetup.com)* - A platform to find and join local groups and events related to personal and professional interests.
3. *LinkedIn (linkedin.com)* - A professional networking platform where you can connect

with like-minded individuals, mentors, and potential collaborators.

Continued Learning and Education:

Consider enrolling in formal courses, workshops, or certifications in areas that align with your goals. Many universities and institutions offer online programs that allow you to acquire new skills and knowledge.